CELLO

THE VERY BEST OF BACH

To access audio visit:
www.halleonard.com/mylibrary

Enter Code
4456-0461-7617-6942

ISBN 978-1-4950-9086-8

7777 W. BLUEMOUND RD. P.O. BOX 13819 MILWAUKEE, WI 53213

In Australia Contact:
Hal Leonard Australia Pty. Ltd.
4 Lentara Court
Cheltenham, Victoria, 3192 Australia
Email: ausadmin@halleonard.com.au

Visit Hal Leonard Online at
www.halleonard.com

ADAGIO
from OBOE CONCERTO IN F MINOR
BWV 1059

By JOHANN SEBASTIAN BACH

CELLO

AIR

from ORCHESTRAL SUITE NO. 3
BWV 1068

By JOHANN SEBASTIAN BACH

CELLO

BIST DU BEI MIR

from NOTEBOOK FOR ANNA MAGDALENA BACH

BWV 508

By GOTTFRIED HEINRICH STÖLZEL

CELLO

BOURRÉE IN E MINOR

from SUITE IN E MINOR FOR LUTE
BWV 996

By JOHANN SEBASTIAN BACH

Cello

INVENTION NO. 4

BWV 775

CELLO

By JOHANN SEBASTIAN BACH

6

INVENTION NO. 14
BWV 785

By JOHANN SEBASTIAN BACH

CELLO

JESU, JOY OF MAN'S DESIRING

from CANTATA 147
BWV 147

By JOHANN SEBASTIAN BACH

CELLO

8

MINUET

from NOTEBOOK FOR ANNA MAGDALENA BACH
BWV Anh. 116

CELLO

Composer Unknown

MINUET IN G MAJOR
from NOTEBOOK FOR ANNA MAGDALENA BACH
BWV Anh. 114

CELLO

By CHRISTIAN PETZOLD

MINUET IN G MINOR

from NOTEBOOK FOR ANNA MAGDALENA BACH
BWV Anh. 115

By CHRISTIAN PETZOLD

CELLO

MUSETTE

from NOTEBOOK FOR ANNA MAGDALENA BACH
BWV Anh. 126

CELLO

Composer Unknown

POLONAISE IN G MINOR

from NOTEBOOK FOR ANNA MAGDALENA BACH
BWV Anh. 119

CELLO

Composer Unknown

SHEEP MAY SAFELY GRAZE

from CANTATA 208
BWV 208

By JOHANN SEBASTIAN BACH

CELLO

SICILIANO
from FLUTE SONATA IN E-FLAT MAJOR
BWV 1031

By JOHANN SEBASTIAN BACH

CELLO

Slowly
Harpsichord

SLEEPERS, AWAKE
(Wachet Auf)
from CANTATA 140
BWV 140

CELLO

By JOHANN SEBASTIAN BACH